D0742104

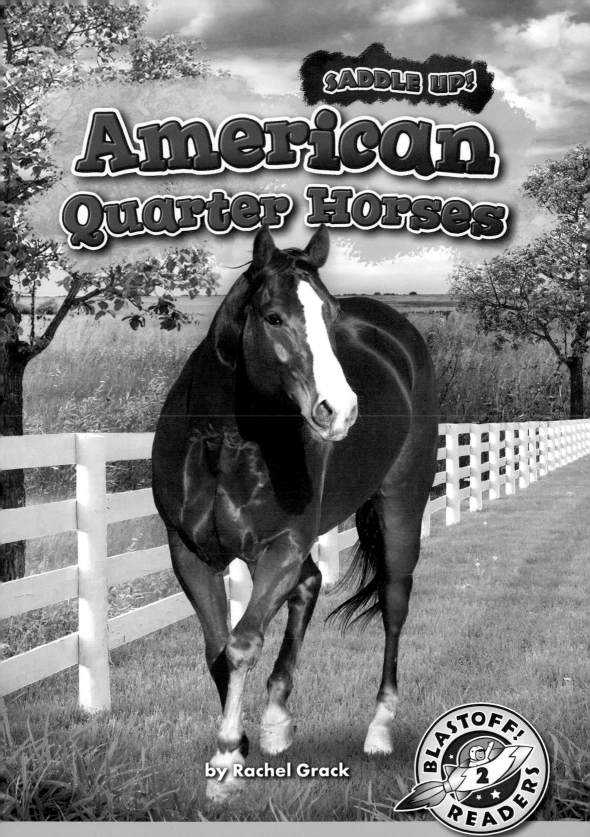

SADDLE UP!

American
Quarter Horses

by Rachel Grack

BLASTOFF!
2
READERS

BELLWETHER MEDIA • MINNEAPOLIS, MN

Blastoff! Readers are carefully developed by literacy experts to build reading stamina and move students toward fluency by combining standards-based content with developmentally appropriate text.

 Level 1 provides the most support through repetition of high-frequency words, light text, predictable sentence patterns, and strong visual support.

 Level 2 offers early readers a bit more challenge through varied sentences, increased text load, and text-supportive special features.

 Level 3 advances early-fluent readers toward fluency through increased text load, less reliance on photos, advancing concepts, longer sentences, and more complex special features.

★ **Blastoff! Universe**

Reading Level

Grade **K**

Grades **1–3**

BLASTOFF! DISCOVERY

Grade **4**

This edition first published in 2021 by Bellwether Media, Inc.

No part of this publication may be reproduced in whole or in part without written permission of the publisher. For information regarding permission, write to Bellwether Media, Inc., Attention: Permissions Department, 6012 Blue Circle Drive, Minnetonka, MN 55343.

Library of Congress Cataloging-in-Publication Data

Names: Koestler-Grack, Rachel A., 1973- author.
Title: American quarter horses / by Rachel Grack.
Description: Minneapolis, MN : Bellwether Media, Inc., 2021. | Series: Blastoff! readers: saddle up! | Includes bibliographical references and index. | Audience: Ages 5-8 | Audience: Grades K-1 | Summary: "Relevant images match informative text in this introduction to American quarter horses. Intended for students in kindergarten through third grade"–Provided by publisher.
Identifiers: LCCN 2019054261 (print) | LCCN 2019054262 (ebook) | ISBN 9781644872321 (library binding) | ISBN 9781618919908 (ebook)
Subjects: LCSH: Quarter horse–Juvenile literature.
Classification: LCC SF293.Q3 K64 2021 (print) | LCC SF293.Q3 (ebook) | DDC 636.1/33–dc23
LC record available at https://lccn.loc.gov/2019054261
LC ebook record available at https://lccn.loc.gov/2019054262

Editor: Elizabeth Neuenfeldt   Designer: Andrea Schneider

Printed in the United States of America, North Mankato, MN.

Table of Contents

Rodeo Stars!

American quarter horses are quick, smart animals.

They can easily **cut** cows from a herd. **Rodeo** crowds love their excellent **cow sense**!

rodeo

Strong and Sturdy

Quarter horses are strong. They have wide chests and thick legs.

Their **hindquarters** are very **muscular**.

hindquarters

Quarter horses stand between 14 and 16 **hands** high.

These strongly built horses can get heavy. They can weigh 1,200 pounds (544 kilograms)!

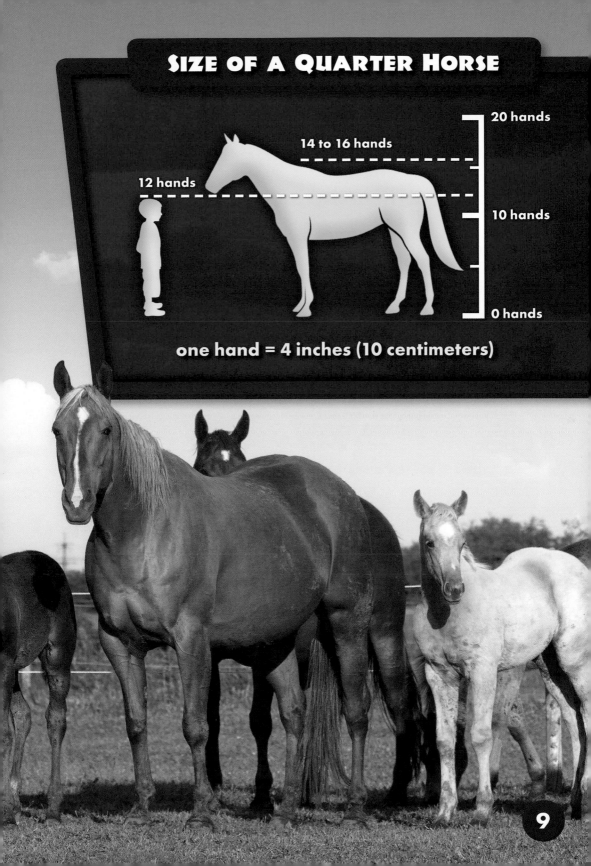

SIZE OF A QUARTER HORSE

20 hands

14 to 16 hands

12 hands

10 hands

0 hands

one hand = 4 inches (10 centimeters)

Quarter horses have 17 different **coat** colors! **Sorrel** is the most common color. Other horses can be black or gray.

COAT COLORS

sorrel

black

gray

Their faces and legs sometimes have white markings.

In 1611, **colonists** in Virginia **bred** farm horses with Spanish horses.

12

The horses could run quarter-mile (0.4-kilometer) races fast! People called them quarter horses.

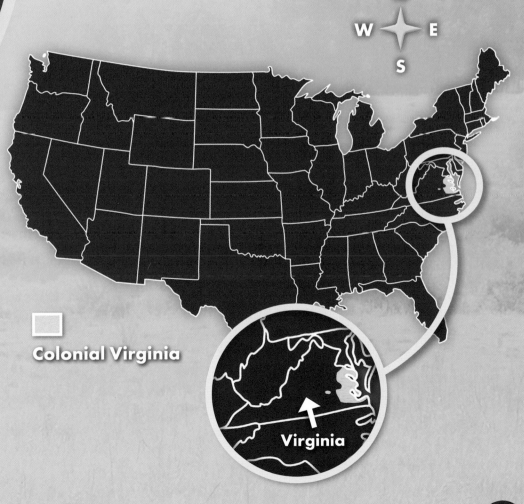

Colonial Virginia

Virginia

Colonists bred quarter horses with Thoroughbreds in 1752. This made even faster horses.

They could run short races at 55 miles (89 kilometers) per hour!

Thoroughbred

quarter horse race
in the 1950s

In the 1800s, quarter horses worked on **cattle drives**. They could round up cows with ease!

cattle drive

AMERICAN QUARTER HORSE TIMELINE

1611
Colonists breed farm horses with Spanish horses

1752
Colonists breed quarter horses with Thoroughbreds

1800s
Cowboys use quarter horses on cattle drives

1940
The American quarter horse becomes an official breed

The **breed** became **official** in 1940.

A Favorite Breed

quarter horse races

Today, quarter horses still race. Their speed and grace shine at the rodeo, too.

These horses can master many events. They can quickly stop and make sharp turns!

QUARTER HORSE RACES

1 mile = 1,760 yards (1,609 meters)

short sprint
220 to 350 yards
(201 to 320 meters)

long sprint
400 to 660 yards
(366 to 604 meters)

distance sprint
770 to 1,000 yards
(704 to 914 meters)

Quarter horses are one of the most popular horse breeds. They are loved by riders around the world.

Their speed and strength
are hard to beat!

Glossary

bred—purposely mated two horses to make horses with certain qualities

breed—a certain type of horse

cattle drives—events in which large herds of cattle move by trail from one place to another

coat—the hair or fur covering an animal

colonists—people who settle in a new place; some colonists from England settled in Virginia during the 1600s.

cow sense—a natural ability to read a cow's behavior and control its actions

cut—to split cows away from the rest of the herd

hands—the units used to measure the height of a horse; one hand is equal to 4 inches (10 centimeters).

hindquarters—the back legs and muscles of a four-legged animal

muscular—having large and strong muscles; muscles help animals and humans move.

official—publically known

rodeo—a show in which riders perform certain skills on horses

sorrel—a light reddish-brown color

To Learn More

AT THE LIBRARY

Grack, Rachel. *American Paint Horses*. Minneapolis, Minn.: Bellwether Media, 2021.

Meister, Cari. *American Quarter Horses*. Mankato, Minn.: Amicus Ink, 2018.

Parise-Peterson, Amanda. *American Quarter Horses*. North Mankato, Minn.: Capstone Press, 2018.

ON THE WEB

FACTSURFER

Factsurfer.com gives you a safe, fun way to find more information.

1. Go to www.factsurfer.com.

2. Enter "American quarter horses" into the search box and click 🔍.

3. Select your book cover to see a list of related content.

Index

The images in this book are reproduced through the courtesy of: University of Southern California/ Getty Images, front cover (horse), 14-15; Vova Shevchuk, pp. 2, 3, 23 (horseshoes); Photography By Marco/ Alamy, p. 4 (inset); RichLegg, pp. 4-5; BiancaGrueneberg, pp. 6-7; Mark J. Barrett/ Alamy, p. 7; Appygaltb, pp. 8 (inset), 10 (gray); juniors @ wildlife, pp. 8-9; Vera Zinkova, p. 10 (sorrel); WOLFAVNI, p. 10 (black); MichaelaS, pp. 10-11; Juniors Bildarchiv GmbH/ Alamy, pp. 12-13, 14 (inset), 20; North Wind Picture Archives/ Alamy, pp. 16-17; Dave G. Houser/ Alamy, pp. 18-19; Tierfotoagentur/ Alamy, pp. 20-21.